BISHOP &
THE BULLY

Written by Ruso

Illustrated by: Cameron W. Dinger

To order additional copies of this book, contact:
Xlibris
844-714-8691
www.Xlibris.com
Orders@Xlibris.com

Library of Congress Control Number: 2022916866
ISBN: Softcover   978-1-6698-4674-1
         Hardcover   978-1-6698-4676-5
         EBook   978-1-6698-4675-8

Print information available on the last page

Rev. date: 09/23/2022

BISHOP & THE BULLY

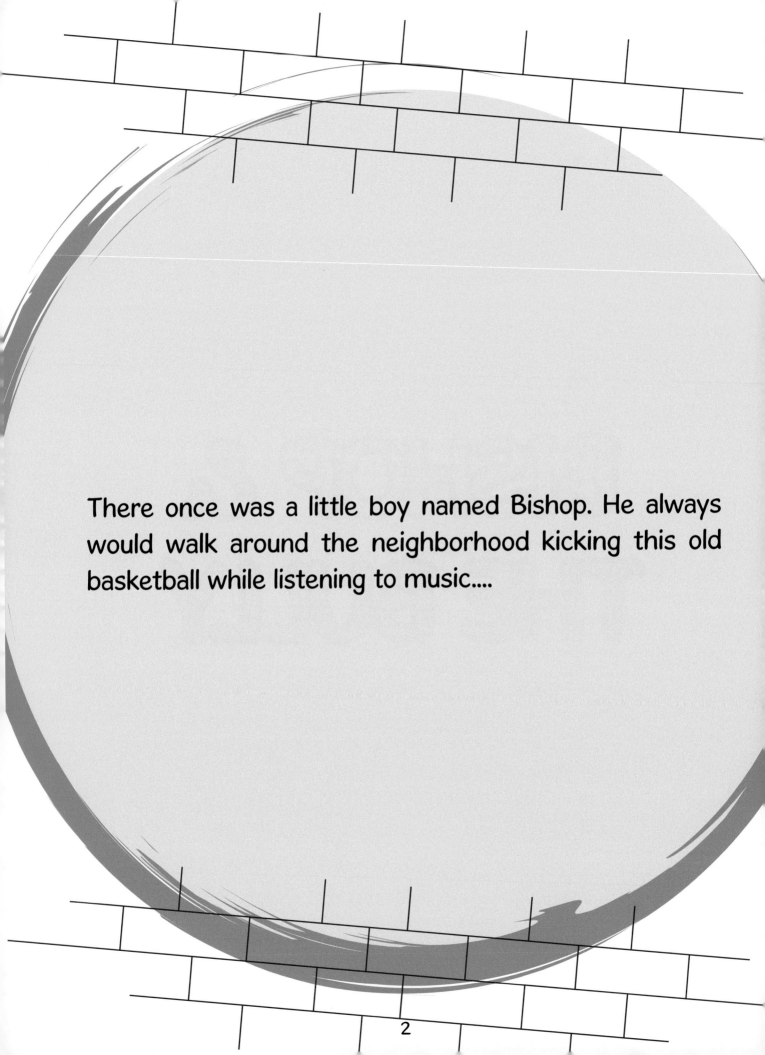

There once was a little boy named Bishop. He always would walk around the neighborhood kicking this old basketball while listening to music....

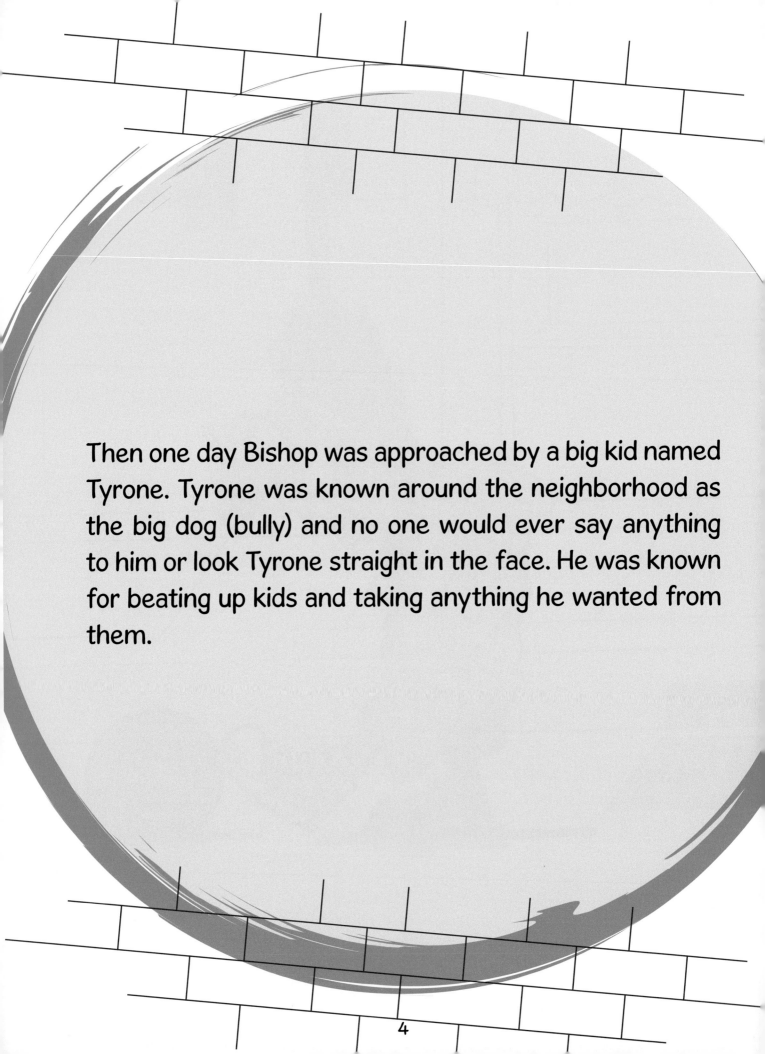

Then one day Bishop was approached by a big kid named Tyrone. Tyrone was known around the neighborhood as the big dog (bully) and no one would ever say anything to him or look Tyrone straight in the face. He was known for beating up kids and taking anything he wanted from them.

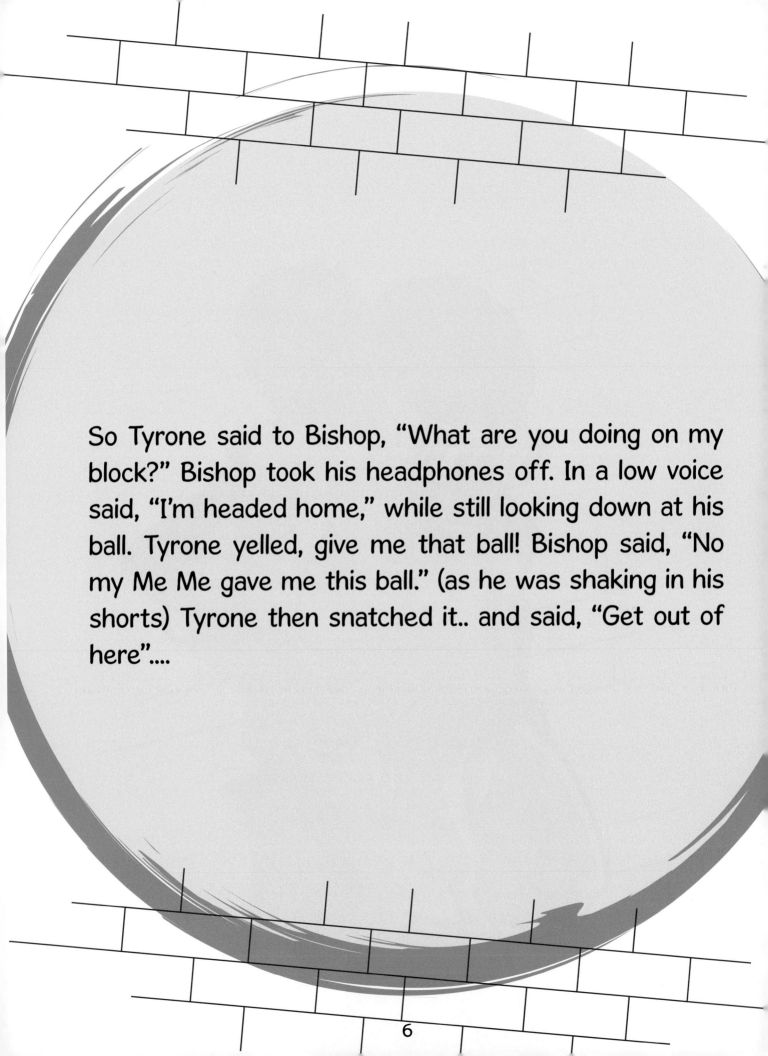

So Tyrone said to Bishop, "What are you doing on my block?" Bishop took his headphones off. In a low voice said, "I'm headed home," while still looking down at his ball. Tyrone yelled, give me that ball! Bishop said, "No my Me Me gave me this ball." (as he was shaking in his shorts) Tyrone then snatched it.. and said, "Get out of here"....

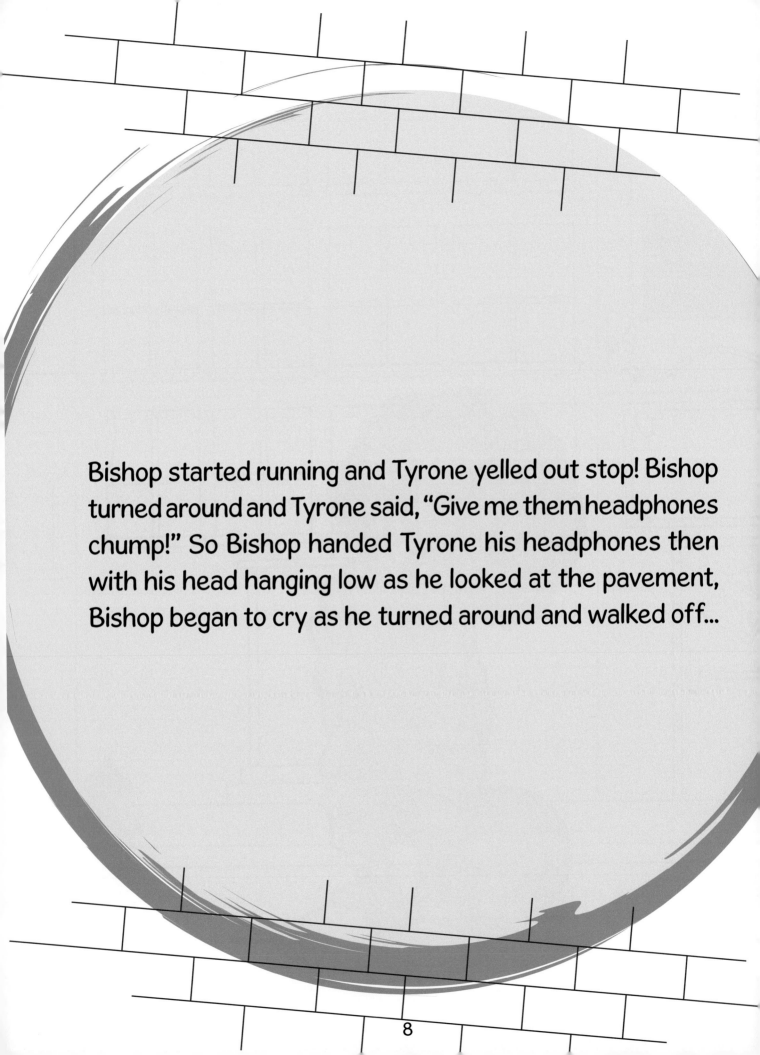

Bishop started running and Tyrone yelled out stop! Bishop turned around and Tyrone said, "Give me them headphones chump!" So Bishop handed Tyrone his headphones then with his head hanging low as he looked at the pavement, Bishop began to cry as he turned around and walked off...

Bishop finally got home and his mother said, "Boy, where have you been?" Bishop said, "Mom I was walking home and this bully took my ball and headphones".. (in a serious voice) Bishop's mom said, "Who is that boy that you are talking about? Do you know his name??," Bishop said, "Yes, it's Tyrone from 115 Street." Bishop, Mom said "Is that over there by the Apollo Theatre?" Yes Ma'am.. Bishop mom said, "Well tomorrow we are going over there to get your stuff back." Bishop said, "No, Mom we can't, he might beat me up…"

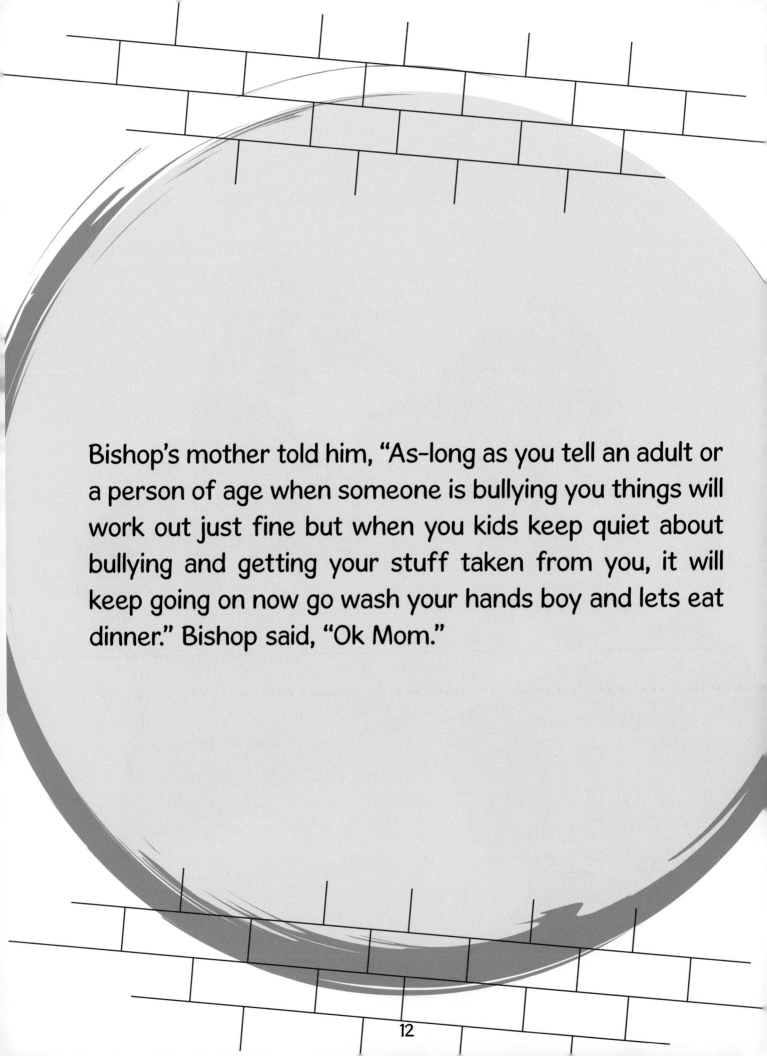

Bishop's mother told him, "As-long as you tell an adult or a person of age when someone is bullying you things will work out just fine but when you kids keep quiet about bullying and getting your stuff taken from you, it will keep going on now go wash your hands boy and lets eat dinner." Bishop said, "Ok Mom."

Like all kids, Bishop had to do his normal chores after dinner. He had to take out the trash, wash dishes and sweep the floor. After about 30 minutes his mom yelled out, "Boy are you done with them chores yet??" Bishop said, "Yes Ma'am." "Well you need to take a bath and brush your teeth, son then you can play your game or watch TV until bedtime..but remember we will be going to 115th Street to get your stuff back tomorrow after church."

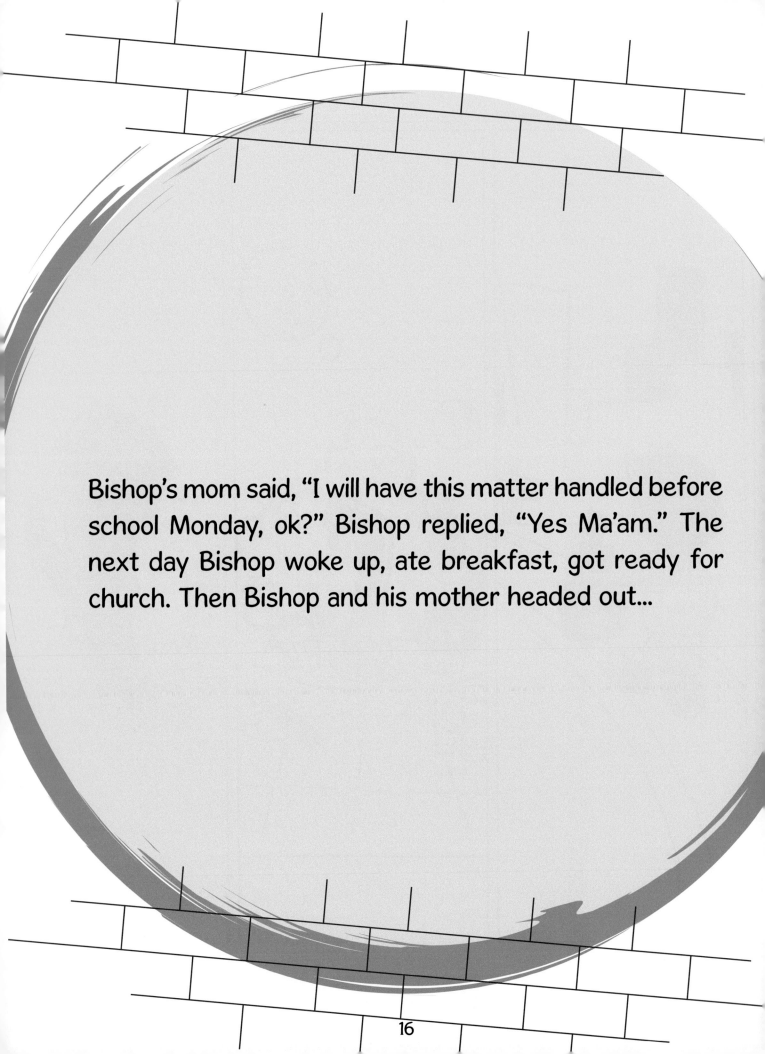

Bishop's mom said, "I will have this matter handled before school Monday, ok?" Bishop replied, "Yes Ma'am." The next day Bishop woke up, ate breakfast, got ready for church. Then Bishop and his mother headed out...

They arrived at church and had a great time. Then it was time for business, as Bishop's mom would say. So they headed out of the sanctuary at church. They got almost to 115th Street and Bishop said, "Mom, I'm feeling sick," as they approached the street with the narrow sidewalk, next to the wall where the bully hangs. His mom said, "Boy If??? You don't stand up and lets go.. We are almost there."

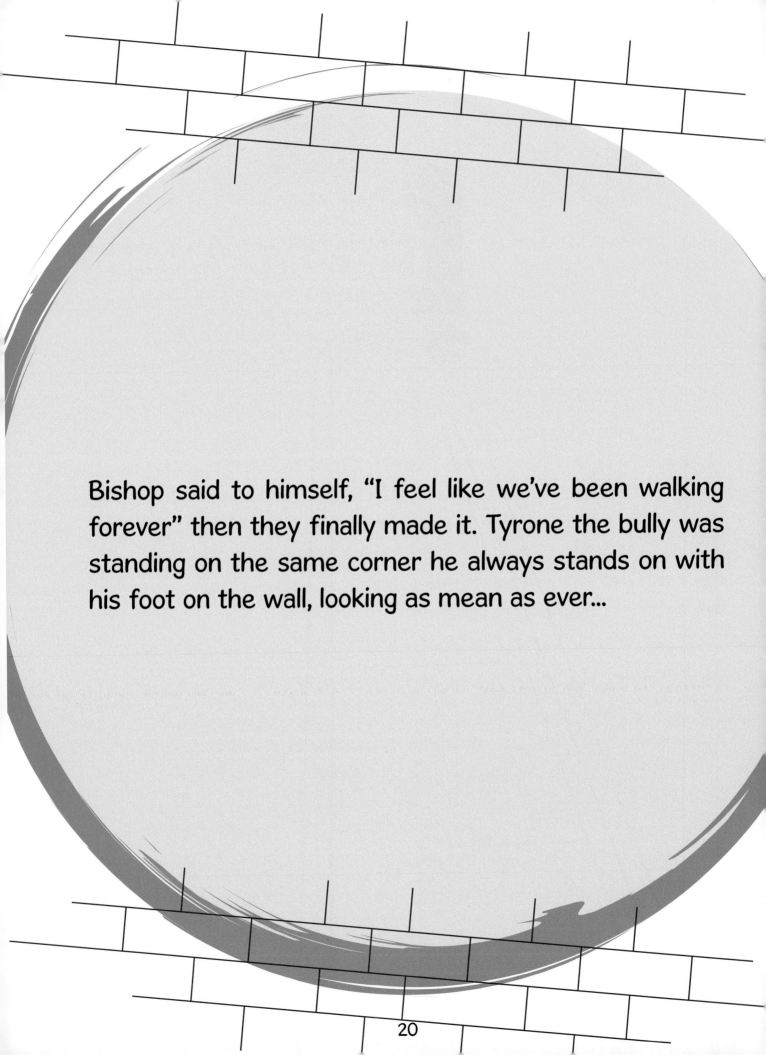

Bishop said to himself, "I feel like we've been walking forever" then they finally made it. Tyrone the bully was standing on the same corner he always stands on with his foot on the wall, looking as mean as ever...

Bishop and his mother walked up. Tyrone said, "Is that you chump?" Bishop's mom answered, "No! And first off he's not a chump and his name is Bishop. I'm his mother and my name is Ms. Annie-May." Tyrone said, "What's the problem?" "I heard you have something that belongs to my son." Tyrone said, "What?" Then Bishop's mother said, "His ball, and I'll take those headphones on your head. They belong to Bishop and where might his ball be son?" Tyrone said, "Right here, well I will take that also.. Yes ma'am" "And hopefully we don't have this problem again." Bishops mom said as he stood across the street with his mouth wide open in disbelief...

Bishops mother asked "What's your last name son?" Tyrone replied Milton. Bishops mother said, "Are you the son of the lady named Mattie that does hair in Harlem off Malcolm X Blvd? And your dad is overseas in the military?" "Yes Ma'am." "Well your mother and I are good friends known each other for along time. I will definitely be getting in contact with her to let her know what you are doing to the neighborhood kids out here on these streets. I know Mattie raised you better than that. Don't you have 6 brothers and 3 sisters?" "Yes Ma'am" "How would you like it if someone was bullying your brother or sisters?" "Not good Ma'am I would be mad." "Well that's what I'm saying. I will be in touch with your mother soon. Good bye son." Bishop and his mother headed home and she gave him along talk about bullying and being in the wrong place at the wrong time...

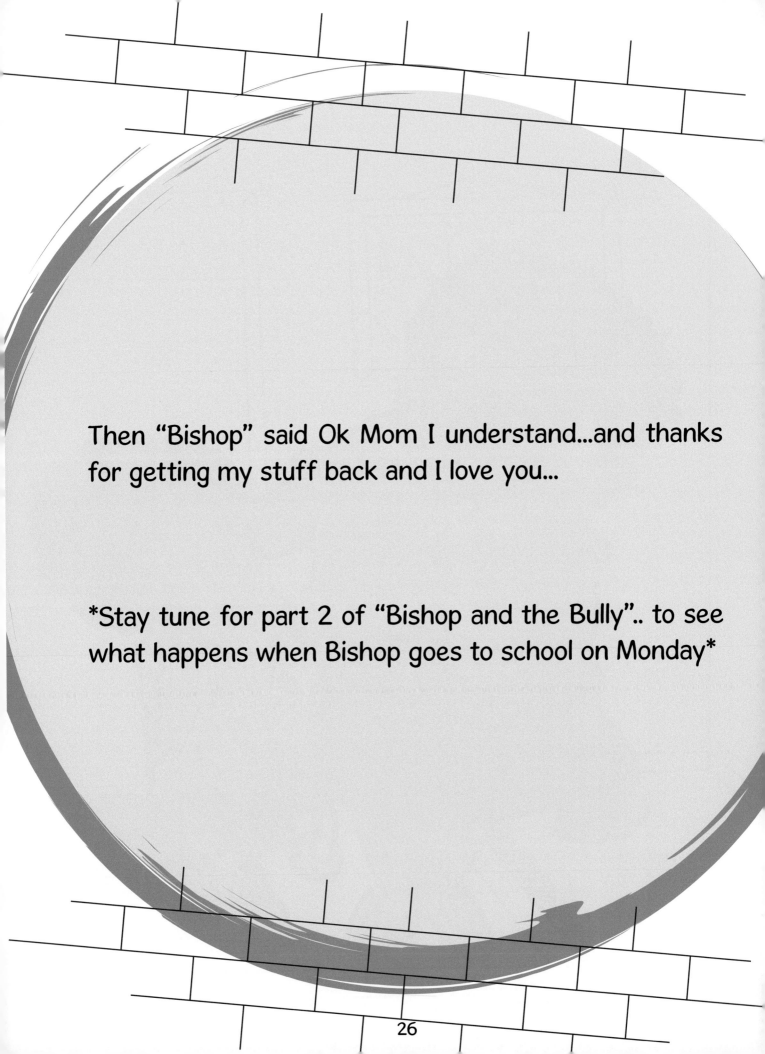

Then "Bishop" said Ok Mom I understand...and thanks for getting my stuff back and I love you...

Stay tune for part 2 of "Bishop and the Bully".. to see what happens when Bishop goes to school on Monday

Was Ruso's inspiration for the "The Bully"

Printed in the United States
by Baker & Taylor Publisher Services